NIAGARA PARKS
Butterflies

Brian McAndrew
Photography by Simon Wilson

JAMES LORIMER & COMPANY LTD., PUBLISHERS
TORONTO, 2000

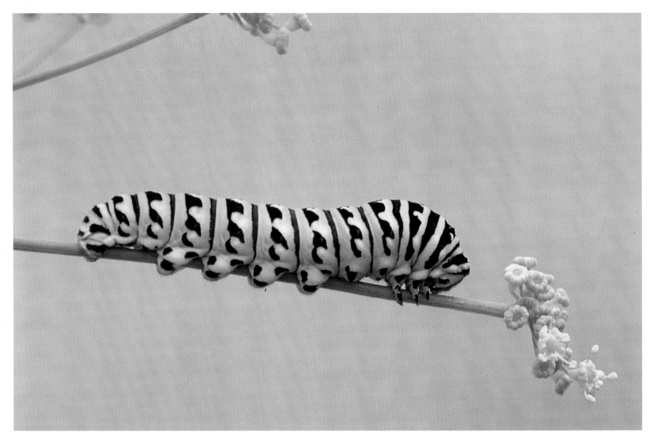

James Lorimer & Company Ltd. acknowledges the support of the Ontario Arts Council. We acknowledge the financial support of the Government of Canada through the Book Publishing Industry Development Program (BPIDP) for our publishing activities. We acknowledge the support of the Canada Council for the Arts for our publishing program.

Cover Photograph: Simon Wilson
Cover design: Kevin O'Reilly
Design and typography: Gwen North

Canadian Cataloguing in Publication Data

McAndrew, Brian
   Niagara Parks Butterflies

Includes index.
ISBN 1-55028-700-1

1. Butterflies – Catalogs and collections – Ontario – Niagara.
2. Niagara Parks Butterfly Conservatory – Catalogs. I. Title

QL545.2.M32 2000   595.78'907371338   C99-932850-6

James Lorimer & Company Ltd., Publishers
35 Britain St.
Toronto, Ontario
M5A 1R7

Acknowledgements

While researching this book, the author was seated on a bench inside the conservatory, making notes, when a visitor paused at his side and asked, "Are you watching the butterflies or watching the people?" It was a perceptive comment.

Occasionally the visitors provide as good a show as the butterflies. There were the two women bobbing and weaving like lightweight boxers through the conservatory, fearful of any meandering butterfly getting too close. Turning to her companion, one whispered through pressed lips, "Be careful not to open your mouth."

And then there was the man baffled by the squawks of the Pharaoh quails, the small birds that eat dead butterflies and spend most of their time hidden in the shrubbery. "Where does that bird sound keep coming from?" he pestered his wife. "It must be a recording coming out of speakers," she replied. "That makes sense," he agreed, as one of the quails darted unnoticed between two bushes at his feet.

Photographer Simon Wilson spent countless days at the conservatory, just after dawn when the building was empty of visitors and the butterflies were starting to stir in order to get the wonderfully colourful pictures for this book. His biggest disappointment about the work was that it ended.

The author and photographer appreciate the guidance of editor Diane Young and the thoughtful contributions of copy editor Laura Ellis.

They are also grateful for the patience, generosity and guidance provided by the conservatory's devoted staff, especially curator Melvin Dell, assistant curator Margaret Pickles, entomologist Cheryl Tyndall, and horticulturists Judy Colley and Jennifer Voogt. The entire staff was a pleasure to work with. This must come from the opportunity to wear shorts every day at work, even in the depths of a Canadian winter.

Contents

Introduction

above
The Niagara Parks Butterfly Conservatory

right
A young visitor encounters a butterfly

Every morning, as the sun rises above the rim of the Niagara Gorge, more than 2,000 butterflies inside the Niagara Parks Butterfly Conservatory unfold their wings in the warmth of the new day and prepare to put on a show.

Opened in late 1996, the conservatory was an instant hit: one of the region's top tourist attractions, it now draws more than 600,000 visitors each year. The numbers are expected to grow, as more visitors to the area discover this modern glass building tucked modestly behind a stand of tall trees, a short drive down river from Niagara Falls.

The conservatory, which showcases 60 butterfly species in a tropical setting, is the largest in North America. It is among a handful of world-class conservatories that include similar facilities in London, Melbourne, Tokyo, and Pine Mountain, Georgia.

It would take a trip around the world to find the many species of colourful butterflies that can be observed fluttering among the conservatory's exotic flowers and trees, pausing to sip nectar and cling to leaves and vines. Most of the butterflies at the conservatory are imported from the tropics. Some are bred and raised within the conservatory's greenhouse. About 30 species occupy the building year round, while others arrive to take up residence according to the season in their country of origin.

"Our show is never exactly the same from one week to another. We're always getting something new in," says conservatory curator Melvin Dell.

Visitors follow a winding 180-metre (600-foot) path leading upwards from the conservatory's ground floor. It takes them past palm trees and fragrant flowers, up to the brink of a waterfall at the highest point in the building. The network of paths ensures the building never feels crowded.

An interpretive staff of 15, more than half the conservatory's workforce, answers questions, identifies butterfly species and plants, and explains why the building contains several birds. (The birds eat dead butterflies.) Staff members are also stationed in the butterfly garden outside the main entrance of the building to explain how the different types of plants attract native butterflies.

The conservatory is one of the Niagara Parks Commission's most innovative projects. The commission is a government-appointed agency responsible for protecting against exploitative development the narrow strip of land running along the Canadian side of the Niagara River between Lake Erie and Lake Ontario.

Since the 1830s, when Niagara Falls first became a tourist destination, there has always been a conflict between the preservation of this natural wonder of the world and crass commercial development. The honky-tonk atmosphere that grew in the immediate vicinity of the falls brought with it widespread criticism. The Niagara Parks Commission was created in 1885 to preserve the natural beauty and dignity of the falls. Commercial attractions still abound, but they are no longer within the park itself.

In 1936, the commission created a school of horticulture and botan-

ical gardens to enhance its operation of the parks. But the botanical gardens were considered incomplete without a tropical-plant conservatory. Plans for a facility devoted exclusively to tropical plants changed quickly after a commission member made a visit to the then largest butterfly conservatory in North America. Located in Pine Mountain, Georgia (near Atlanta), this conservatory is a hugely popular attraction.

Worldwide, there are 166 butterfly conservatories, zoo exhibits, and gardens, including 14 in Canada, 22 in the United States, and 72 in England. While some of these facilities undertake extensive scientific research, the Niagara Parks conservatory is primarily intended to give visitors an opportunity to see exotic creatures from around the globe. It does some modest research

in creating artificial food sources for butterflies and offers educational tours for schools.

"Our purpose here is conservation," says assistant curator Margaret Pickles. "We don't push that message, but we hope it is something people will appreciate once they've gone through the conservatory."

Whatever message visitors take away, observing butterflies is simply an uplifting experience.

This book captures in a series of stunning photographs the beauty of the butterflies, the enchantment of the visitors, and the ingenious design of the conservatory itself. It tells the story of the butterflies and exotic plants and takes a look at the facility's behind-the-scenes operations. Its aim is to enlighten and provide nearly as much enjoyment from words and photos as a visit to the conservatory itself.

Not Just a Pretty Bug

above
A Zebra Longwing

right
An Eggfly larva

There are more of them than us. Way more. Insects account for three-quarters of all animal species in the world. And make no mistake: just because butterflies are pretty and colourful doesn't change the fact that they are, indeed, bugs. But what bugs!

Butterflies, along with moths, belong to an order of insect known as *Lepidoptera,* meaning "scaled wings." Like all insects, they have six legs, one pair of antennae, a head, thorax, and abdomen. There are somewhere around 160,000 known species, with new ones still being discovered in remote tropical regions of the world. About 20,000 of these species are butterflies and the remainder are moths.

By far, the majority of butterfly species are found in the tropical countries of Asia, South America, Central America, and Africa. But they range throughout the globe from Australia to Finland. In more temperate climates, including much of Europe and North America, butterflies exist only during the summer. There are no butterflies in the extremely cold regions of the world, such as the Arctic and Antarctic.

North America has an abundance of butterflies, but most species are found in the southern regions. Mexico boasts more than 2,000 species, and there are 575 species in the United States. Canada makes do with 275 species.

Before winter arrives, some butterflies, like the familiar orange-and-black Monarch found in all 10 Canadian provinces and the northern United States, begin migrations to the south. The Monarch is one of the few butterflies that have been studied extensively in the north and while wintering in the remote mountainous regions of Mexico. Little is known, however, about the southern treks of other species such as the Sulphur, Mourning Cloak and Question Mark.

Some butterfly populations that die off during the winter are replaced by others, like the Cloudless Sulphur,

Little Yellow, Gulf Fritillary, Painted Lady, Red Admiral and Common Buckeye, that move north from the southern United States, Mexico and Central America.

Moths and butterflies are distinct from each other. Butterflies are more colourful, fly by day, and have a club-shaped end to their antennae. Moths move about at night, have dull colours, and, if you get up close enough to look, have tapered or feathery antennae.

BUTTERFLY EVOLUTION

Butterflies have been around for a long time. Their fossils have been found in 30-million-year-old shale deposits, which, on the evolutionary scale, makes them fairly recent in terms of life forms. The fossils resemble quite closely the butterflies we see today.

Scientists believe butterflies have a much longer history, evolving from Scorpion Flies, which were around 250 million years ago. Their biggest evolutionary phase may have begun 90 million years ago when flowering plants, which supply the butterfly's nectar food supply, began to emerge.

The biggest known butterfly over those millions of years was likely no bigger than the Atlas Moth, the largest of its kind today. The wingspan of the Atlas Moth can reach 30 centimetres (12 inches). Found in Malaysia and other Southeast Asian countries, the Atlas Moth is found only occasionally in the conservatory. As an adult, it has no mouth and does not feed. It lives only a few days, just long enough to mate and lay eggs.

The butterfly's body is covered with a protective armour known as chitin, which forms the exoskeleton — a skeleton on the outside — and by a layer of small scales, giving the insect its soft appearance and colours.

The head contains a proboscis, a tongue-like tube that draws liquid nectar from flowering plants. The butterfly has no jaws, nose, or lungs. The antennae are used for balance and smell. The body organs absorb oxygen directly from a crude air tube, which may be the reason butterflies have never become any larger than their current size.

The two bulging compound eyes can detect shapes and movement from a number of different angles but do not see colour in the same way we do. Instead, the eyes are much more sensitive to ultraviolet light.

A butterfly has two pairs of wings, which overlap between the front and rear of the body. The visible hollow tubes that create a frame for the wings are veins. Since butterflies are cold-blooded, they are often seen first thing in the morning on a warm rock, with wings extended, absorbing the heat so they can fly. Butterflies are less active on cool and cloudy days.

The scales on the wing serve various purposes. Male butterflies have specialized "scent scales" that give off an odour when they flutter around females, trying to attract a mate. And it is the scales that help give the butterfly its colours and make it so popular.

Butterflies create pigments that give them blackish brown colours. Some of their creams and yellows

result from the plant leaves consumed during the caterpillar stage. The most brilliant colours, however, come from the scales. The translucent scales contain long, rib-like ridges and act like a prism to refract light. The shades of colour can vary as the wings move and the angle of the light striking the scales changes. This creates the shimmering effect best displayed in flight by the stunning Blue Morpho.

Touch a butterfly, and the scales rub off in what looks like dust. Preserving the scales is one reason why we shouldn't touch butterflies.

STAGES OF LIFE

There are four stages in the life of a butterfly: egg, larva, pupa, and adult. Butterfly eggs are laid in clusters of anywhere from 5 to 100 depending on the species. The small, round eggs are laid on or near the plant that will provide a food source once they hatch and become caterpillars, a phase known as the larva stage. The larva eats its way out of the egg and then devours the remainder of the egg for its first source of nutrition before moving on to eating plant leaves.

A caterpillar is made up of an eyeless head and a pair of toothed jaws attached to a 13-segment trunk. As it grows, the caterpillar sheds its skin four or five times during this major feeding stage. It also creates large — by caterpillar standards — amounts of excrement, known as frass.

Slow-moving and vulnerable, the caterpillar protects itself from preda-tors through the use of camouflaging colour, making it resemble a tree leaf, and with fierce-looking false "eyes" and spines on its back.

As it enters the pupa, or cocoon, stage, the caterpillar's skin shrivels and splits and forms the chrysalis, the pod-like phase before becoming an adult butterfly. The caterpillar spins a small piece of silk that the chrysalis uses to attach itself to a tree branch or other secure hiding spot.

Inside the chrysalis, the creature essentially melts into a puddle of chemicals and recreates itself as a butterfly. "There's a magical mystery that we can't see that is going on inside," says conservatory entomolo-gist Cheryl Tyndall. "That's what is special about the butterfly. It's a fairy-tale kind of creature."

When this metamorphosis is complete, the skin of the pupa splits, and the head, legs, and antennae slowly appear from inside the case. After a short rest, the remainder of the body emerges along with the soft, wet, and crumpled wings.

The butterfly hangs upside down, allowing blood to flow into veins in the wings which, in turn, allows the wings to expand to their full size. After the butterfly dries and its chitin armour hardens, it is ready to fly off as a fully mature adult.

Butterflies live pretty short lives. A butterfly with a high-energy diet of sugary plant nectar will live about two weeks. Some of the Long-Wing butterflies that include pollen in their diets can live as long as three or four months.

A pupae shipment

Spectacular Species

Half of the more than 60 species of butterflies on exhibit at the conservatory are found only during certain times of the year. These are the 30 most common or popular species that occupy the tropical environment inside the conservatory. They are identified by their common name, followed by the scientific name. They have been grouped by colour to make their identification easier.

A Tiger Longwing

Red Lacewing
Cethosia biblis

Oddly, the vibrant colours on this butterfly make it more difficult for predators to detect. The Red Lacewing displays a blaze of colour, ranging from an intense orange at the front of the closed wings to a pale yellow and rusty orange, interlaced by lines of brown and black. This brilliant array serves to disguise the common triangular shape of a butterfly at rest, when it is most vulnerable to attack. The bright red on the inside of the wings, framed by a black outline, also cries out for attention. The message is not pleasant. It is a warning to predators that the Red Lacewing may be pretty to look at, but tastes awful. The foul flavour comes from the poisonous spines the species uses as a protective cover during its caterpillar stage. The Red Lacewing is found in the Philippines and Malaysia and has a wingspan of 9 centimetres (3 1/2-inches).

Small Postman
Heliconius erato

The Small Postman is found all across Central America and South America, but it is to Trinidad that it owes its memorable name. This popular butterfly, ranging in size from 5 to 8 centimetres (2 to 3 inches), is easily seen at the conservatory because it flies low to the ground, usually at eye level. It is distinguished by two swatches of red near the tip of the open wing, with a yellow stripe across the middle of the black wings. In Trinidad, the postal carriers wear dark uniforms with red epaulettes and a yellow stripe up the side of the pant legs. Like other types of *Heliconius*, the male Small Postman is aggressive and mates with the female while she is still in the chrysalis. It plants a chemical in the female's abdomen to prevent any other males from also mating with her. During the summer months, the Small Postman occasionally flies as far north as southern Texas.

Rumanzovia Swallowtail
Papilio rumanzovia

Just try to pick this butterfly out in a crowd. It is fairly large at 10 centimetres (4 inches) wide and has impressive colours. The only problem is that this swallowtail comes in a wide variety of colours. The background colour of the wings can be solid black, grey, or white. It may have a splash of red running down the inside edge of each wing next to the body. Or it may not. It could also have bits of orange on the back of the wing, along with some white. No matter what the colour, it will always have a red eyespot on the back of the hindwing. First discovered in the Philippines, it is found in most parts of Asia.

Cattleheart
Parides iphidamus

Throughout Central America and South America, the Cattleheart can be found in habitats ranging from tropical forests to wide-open plains. It is about 10 centimetres (4 inches) wide, and the male and female of the species have similar patterns but different colours. Both have rich black wings, with a sliver of yellow spotting along the edges and two red patches on the back of each wing. On the forewings, the males have green spots, while the female's are white. Predators learn to stay away from the Cattleheart because of a poisonous taste it acquires during the caterpillar stage by feeding on Aristolochia, a toxic vine.

Julia

Dryas iulia

This butterfly tends to flit more than it flutters. Basking in the sun, the wings of the Julia are a pumpkin shade of orange, with a bit of black at the front of the forewing. The closed wings have a mottled brown appearance, with many narrow veins. These butterflies gather in large clusters and feed on the nectar of flowers, plant sap, and the "honeydew" left on plants by pests such as aphids. The Julia is found in Central America and South America, and is bred at the conservatory, accounting for their large numbers. It has the ability to fly about rapidly and has a wingspan of about 7 centimetres (2 3/4 inches).

Plain Tiger

Danaus chrysippus

A slightly smaller cousin of the favourite North American butterfly, the Monarch, this species is a paler orange, with thinner black ribs and spots. Its wingspan does not exceed 8 centimetres (3 inches). In India and Malaysia it goes by the name of Plain Tiger but is known in Africa as the African Monarch. The caterpillar feeds on milkweed, giving it protection against predators that do not like the taste of the plant's poisonous properties. The butterfly also has an obnoxious odour. Its bright colour and slow flight help advertise its formidable method of self-defence. The Plain Tiger can also be found in Australia.

Gulf Fritillary

Agraulis vanillae

Also known as the Silver-spotted Flambeau, this butterfly sometimes travels as far north as the Great Lakes from Mexico and the southern United States. It ranges throughout Central America and South America, and has a wingspan of between 6 and 7 centimetres (2 1/4- and 2 3/4-inches). It has silver spots on the underwings, and the deep orange background warns predators that it is poisonous, having fed on the toxic passion vine as a caterpillar.

Banded Orange
Dryadula phaetusa

The range of this butterfly crosses all of Central America and South America, but the Banded Orange in the conservatory reproduce locally in an on-site breeding program. They can be found coupling or roosting in palm trees, displaying bands of cocoa brown, white, and orange across their closed wings. But opened to its full 7-centimetre (2 3/4-inch) width, the butterfly looks as if someone has swept a paintbrush loaded with bright orange paint across its brown back. The bright colour is a warning that the butterfly is unpalatable. They fly slowly and are easy to spot, returning over and over again to roost in clumps in familiar spots. Because of a relatively long life and the ease with which they can be bred, they are popular in butterfly research programs.

Tiger Longwing
Heliconius hecale

Found anywhere from tropical rainforests to open pastures throughout Central America and South America, the Tiger Longwing has a forewing that is wider (8 centimetres or 3 inches) than that of most other longwings. Its colouring is varied. It can be entirely black on the forewing, in contrast to the orange near the middle where the wings connect to the body, with white patches closer to the ends of the wings. It feeds on flower nectar and pollen and vigorously chases away any other butterfly in the vicinity. Other butterflies hoping to avoid predators mimic the colouring of the Tiger Longwing, a member of the poisonous *Heliconius* genus. Scientists have discovered that the copycat butterflies can be distinguished from the Tiger Longwing because they fly at different elevations in the rainforest canopy and find separate roosting spaces at night.

Great Orange Tip
Hebomoia glaucippe

Looks can be deceiving. That's important in the world of survival. With its 10-centimetre- (4-inch-) wide wings folded up, the Great Orange Tip looks like a torn piece of a brown paper bag — the better to blend in with dead leaves. When the butterfly's wings are wide open, its name speaks for itself. The translucent white wings are tipped with bright orange, along with a narrow band of dark brown around the edges. The colour comes from the combination of a red pigment in the butterfly's scales and violet shades of light reflected in the structure of the wing. This can make photographing the Great Orange Tip difficult because some films cannot pick up the hidden red pigment. Although a plentiful species in its native Malaysia, with a range that extends throughout southeast Asia, the Great Orange Tip remains out of sight much of the time, as it flies through the forest canopy of tall trees.

The Queen

Danaus gilippus

Another cousin of the Monarch, this butterfly is smaller in size at 7 centimetres (2 3/4-inches) wide but has a much more vivid orange colour. Its white spots also stand out in greater contrast to the deeper orange hues of both the open and closed wings. It lacks the Monarch's black-coloured veins on the opened wings. The Queen is native to Florida but can be found in some other southern states as well as Mexico, Central America, and South America. It occasionally flies with the Monarch but does not migrate as far. The Queen cannot survive cold weather, so its range is limited to the warmer regions.

During the summer, the Queen migrates north to the United States but does not reverse the route in the winter. Like all members of the *Danaidae* family, it is a strong flyer, although the translucence of its wings gives it a fragile appearance.

Clipper
Parthenos sylvia

The best way to identify the Clipper is by looking at its body. Black and orange bands wrap around the body, in patterns similar to a wasp's. The wings are a complex blending of colours and come in two different forms. In both, the tips of the forewings are black, with a band of white spots. The most common in the conservatory is the brown Clipper. Much of the wing is covered in a brown and dull orange colour similar to the hide of a tiger. A rare type of Clipper has a predominantly blue background. The Clipper was first found in the Solomon Islands, but it is also native to much of Asia. The Clipper has a 10-centimetre (4-inch) wingspan and moves erratically in flight.

Owl
Caligo illioneus

Among the largest of South American butterflies, the Owl has a 12- to 15-centimetre (4 3/4- to 6-inch) wingspan. Large enough to cover the palm of an adult's hand, this butterfly is more likely to land on a visitor's back or shoulder. Although dull brown in colour, its size and distinctive yellow-rimmed eyespot resembling the eye of an owl make it easy to find. The shimmering colours of the opened wings vary from light blue to vivid purple. Often it is the first butterfly spotted in the conservatory. The eyespot acts to frighten away predators or to divert their attention away from the vulnerable body. An attacking bird will usually peck at the eyespot, giving the Owl a chance to escape, battered but alive. This species is fond of bananas and can often be found feeding at the conservatory's fruit trays. The 12-centimetre- (4 3/4-inch-) long caterpillars can cause enormous damage to a banana plant.

Atlas Moth
Attacus atlas

With a wingspan of between 11 and 30 centimetres (4 1/2- and 12 inches), the Atlas is the largest moth in the world. Clear patches on its brown wings give it the appearance of having holes but act as camouflage when it is resting against a tree trunk. The moth is nocturnal; during the day, it usually rests on trees or rocks. The moth has no mouth and does not eat. It lives just long enough — a few days at most — to mate and lay eggs.

Zebra Longwing

Heliconius charitonius

This butterfly's name says it all. Its wings are long and narrow, a description applicable to several different types of longwing butterflies. The bright yellow stripes on a black background warn predators to avoid this species at all costs. The caterpillars absorb a poison from feeding on passion vines that is passed along to the butterfly. The adults are among the most passionate of butterflies; they thrive in captivity and breed rapidly. They were among the first butterflies used in the conservatory's on-site breeding program. The male Zebra Longwing is so aggressive that it engages in "pupal mating," the act of coupling with a female while she is still in the pupal stage. The 7-centimetre- (2 3/4-inch-) wide Zebra Longwing is native to Costa Rica and found throughout Central America and South America.

Sulphur
Phoebis sennae

Given the brilliant yellow colour of the Large Orange Sulphur and Cloudless Sulphur, these butterflies have an appropriate name. Although the female can be white, both have black specks along the edge of the wings. The Sulphur was originally discovered in Brazil and ranges between Argentina and the southern United States. During the months of August and September, it will fly to the northern states but is unable to reproduce after the journey. It is among the easiest butterflies to spot in the open because, in addition to its startling colour, it lives in parks, gardens, fields, and beaches. The relatively small Sulphur ranges in size from 6 to 8 centimetres (2 to 3 inches). The males fly around rapidly in search of a mate.

Grecian Shoemaker

Catonephele numilia

Don't be confused by the name. These butterflies that can resemble a withered leaf when resting on a vine were first discovered in Brazil. Rotting fruit is the favoured food. They can be found around the fruit trays in the conservatory although they most often prefer to dwell deeply in the shade away from direct sunlight. As a defence, the female Grecian Shoemaker takes on the appearance of other butterflies that feed on toxic plants and impart a bad taste on predators, without actually producing the bilious flavour itself. The butterfly is dull in appearance with its 7.5 centimetre (3 inch) wide wings folded. It boasts pastel yellow patches on its opened upper wings and can have bright reddish-orange and black rear wings.

Giant Swallowtail
Papilio cresphontes

This large butterfly, ranging in size from 10 to 14 centimetres (4 to 5 1/2 inches), likes to spread its wings and fly. Although most common in Central America, Mexico, and the southern United States, it occasionally makes its way to southern Ontario. It is the largest butterfly found in North America. Like many swallowtails, the young caterpillar looks like a bird dropping, which keeps it safe from predators. It turns a green colour to blend in with the surrounding foliage of its host citrus plants. This caterpillar can wreak havoc on a citrus grove. Aside from its size, the Giant Swallowtail is distinguished by a pale yellow line across the back of its formidable black wings, as well as a yellow outline along the lower edge of the wings, ending in two red dots above a yellow dot on each of its two tails.

Tailed Jay
Graphium agamemnon

Also known as the Green Spotted Triangle, this fairly large butterfly, with a 10-centimetre (4-inch) wingspan, is one of the few species that are green. Green spots run up the back of the closed wings on a light brown background, while the open wings display a lime green spotted pattern against a green-black background. This colouring allows the Tailed Jay to blend in well in the green tropical rain forests of its native Malaysia and other parts of southeast Asia. The species is also known as a Kite Swallowtail because the narrow, pointed wings give it the appearance of a kite. It belongs to the butterfly family *Papilionidae*, which is characterized by a structure imbedded behind the head of the caterpillar, known as an "osmeterium." This brightly coloured and foul-smelling forked horn can be raised to scare off predators.

Malachite
Siproeta stelenes

The Malachite is aptly named after the semiprecious gemstone its colouring resembles. Its opened wings are splashed with bright green against a black background. This appearance gives the Malachite the ability to conceal itself in the shadows of the forests. The green colour fades in the bright sunlight.

The Malachite feeds on rotting fruit and will soar in a slow and lazy flight pattern high into the canopy of the forest to reach food. It was discovered in Honduras but has a range between southern Texas and South America. The Malachite was found in Florida for the first time in the 1960s; it was believed to have migrated there from Cuba. This remarkably pretty butterfly has a wingspan of between 8 and 10 centimetres (3 to 4 inches.)

Blue and White Longwing
Heliconius cydno

This graceful and slow-moving butterfly appears to surf on air waves rather than fly. It has a rich white colour over a sapphire blue background on each of its forewings. A pair of red bands appears on the edge of the wings when the butterfly is at rest with its wings closed. It can reach a width of 9 centimetres (3 1/2 inches) and is found in Central America and South America. While feeding on pollen, both males and females stand guard against any intrusion by other butterflies. Researchers are still trying to determine why this butterfly may have as many as four different variations in its colour patterns, all of which are designed to warn predators that the Blue and White Longwing is unpalatable. Its nasty taste is the result of poisons absorbed from passion vines it fed on as a caterpillar.

Blue Morpho
Morpho peleides

Morpho means "beautiful" in Latin, and this large, lovely butterfly easily lives up to its name. The shimmering blue colour of the opened wings is created as rays of sunlight bounce off ridges of scales on the butterfly's broad, 12-centimetre (4 3/4-inch) back. The Blue Morpho is easily one of the favourite butterflies among visitors to the conservatory. They are not alone. The Blue Morpho was prized by collectors and popular in jewellery until those practices fell into disfavour in recent years. The only Blue Morphos available to the conservatory are from butterfly farms in the butterfly's native Costa Rica and other parts of Central America and South America. One of the reasons for its enormous popularity among collectors was its intense blue colour that never faded because it resulted from reflected light rather than pigment. The bright blue colour changes to dark brown once the butterfly leaves the sunlight for protective cover beneath trees and is a method of shaking off trailing predators. The Blue Morpho feeds on fruit and is often seen around the fruit trays in the conservatory, where it is sometimes confused with the Owl species. The Owl has one eyespot visible on its closed wings, while the Blue Morpho has several eyespots against a brown background.

Great Eggfly
Hypolimnas bolina

A deep, soft blue in colour, the male of this species has white, egg-like spots on its open wings that reflect a purplish blue shade when struck at different angles by the light. The female is larger than the male and is often brown in colour, with a different pattern of white spots and two orange dots, one on each of the open wings. The Great Eggfly, whose wingspan ranges from 7 to 11 centimetres (2 3/4 to 4 1/2 inches), is native to Malaysia and can be found in the South Pacific and Australia. In 1984 the tiny island republic of Nauru, near Papua New Guinea and the Solomon Islands, featured the Great Eggfly on a pair of postage stamps. The Great Eggfly is bred at the conservatory. The caterpillar feeds on the sweet potato, while the butterfly favours the Lantana plant and is also found around the conservatory's fruit trays.

Common Mormon
Papilio polytes

Given its name, you might think the Common Mormon would make its home in the western United States, possibly in Utah. But no. Outside of conservatories, the Common Mormon is typically found in Southeast Asia, especially in China, Japan, Sri Lanka, and India. A deep black colour, the male butterfly has a band of yellow across the back of its wings, with yellow spotting on the wings' edges. The female has three different patterns of colour. While the male is a faster flier, the female protects itself with colours similar to another type of swallowtail that is poisonous to predators. The Common Mormon is bred at the conservatory and reaches a size of 10 centimetres (4 inches).

Doris Longwing

Heliconius doris

This butterfly lives throughout Central America and South America and displays a variety of colourings, depending on where it is found. It ranges in size from 6 to 10 centimetres (2 1/4 to 4 inches). The front wings are always black with white markings, but the rear wings can be either orange, blue, or green.

Kotzobuea Swallowtail
Pachliopta kotzebuea

This is one of the most remarkable butterflies in the conservatory. It is nearly pure black in colour, with a touch of reddish orange at the rear of the body and on the head. A close look reveals that the black colouring is so dense it has the appearance of crushed velvet. The Kotzebuea Swallowtail is distinguished from other swallowtails by the two round protrusions on its tail. It is the only one of 15 members of the Pachliopta butterfly genus living in the conservatory. Kotzebuea have a large range throughout the tropical regions of the world, from India, Sri Lanka, and the Philippines to Ecuador, Guatemala, and Peru. They are powerful fliers, with wings about 9 centimetres (3 1/2 inches) wide.

Mosaic
Colobura dirce

It is hard to tell if the Mosaic is coming or going. Its complex pattern gives it the appearance of having two heads. The black stripes against the light background of the wings point toward the eyespot on the false head, creating a further deception. If attacked by a bird, the Mosaic might lose part of its wing but is still able to fly away. Ranging throughout Central America and South America, the Mosaic has a wingspan of 5 to 7 centimetres (2 to 2 3/4 inches).

Rice Paper

Idea leuconoe

These large butterflies, up to 10 centimetres (4 inches) in width, lope along in a lazy flight pattern that gives them the appearance of sailing. Native to Malaysia and found throughout India, the South Pacific, and Australia, this butterfly's transparent, tissue-like wings have earned it the name Rice Paper, although it is also known as the Large Tree Nymph. It will fly just below the tree canopy in the tropical rain-forest, but is mostly found around mangrove swamps. Its toxic body fluids provide a protection against attack, similar to the defence used by the Monarch, a cousin of the Rice Paper. The waxy-looking pupa is suspended head down from a silken pad and, like other members of the Danaidae family of butter-flies, often has either bright gold or silver spots.

Cracker
Hamadryas februa

While some of the Cracker butterflies contain bright markings, others, like the Gray Cracker, are among the plainest butterflies in a world of incredible colours. In either the closed or opened-wing position, the Gray Cracker is distinguished by its mottled browns ranging from beige near the body to muddy-river brown around the edges. The rear wing contains several small white eyespots rimmed in brown. The colourings are useful as camouflage against tree trunks. Ironically, it belongs to a family of butterflies, *Nymphalidae*, that is one of the largest with thousands of wildly colourful members. The Cracker, a type of butterfly from Mexico with a wingspan of 7 centimetres (2 3/4 inches) makes a cracking sound when it darts out at other insects or people.

White Peacock
Anartia jatrophae

This small butterfly has a wingspan of just 5 centimetres (2 inches) and a complicated pattern across the back of its wings. The background on the wings consists of various shades of purplish blue, with a zigzag orange-and-brown fringe around the edges. There are three well-separated dark dots on each wing. The White Peacock is native to Mexico but can be found throughout Texas and the deep south of the United States, along with Central America and South America. During warm summer months, it will migrate as far north as Massachusetts. It can be found near swamps, around wet and weedy fields, on the edges of ponds, and along streams and ditches. Despite its ability to travel long distances, the White Peacock is not considered to be an especially strong flyer.

Behind the Scenes

above
*Horticulturist Jennifer Voogt trims
a Butterfly Bush*

right
*A conservatory entomologist
handles a pupa*

A great deal of activity goes on behind the scenes at the conservatory. Most visitors get just a tiny peek at the facility's inner workings through the "emergence window," where pupae are pinned to a sheet of corkboard and suspended in the picture-window display case. As the butterfly inside struggles to free itself from its casing, enthralled visitors watch attentively.

Behind the emergence window, visitors can look down into the conservatory's laboratory, where much of the work is done to prepare the pupae for display. Here pupae are collected from the breeding stations in the rear greenhouse, ship-

ments of imported pupae are unpacked, and the entomology staff keep a close watch for any pupae infected by disease or parasites, which, if left unattended, could threaten the existence of every butterfly in the conservatory.

There is much more that most visitors never get to see. Horticultural staff arrive at dawn to water and trim the conservatory plants. Butterflies have a very short life, with most living just a few weeks. Each morning brings the task of sweeping up the butterflies that have perished overnight. Trays are filled daily with rotting fruit to nourish several types of butterflies, such as the Blue Morpho, and to provide a location where visitors can watch these species feed and rest.

Since the life cycle of the butterfly is so short, the conservatory runs its own breeding program in addition to importing species from tropical butterfly farms. Research is being done on an artificial diet for caterpillars. And there is an ongoing battle to eliminate unwanted bugs without the use of pesticides.

THE BREEDING PROGRAM
The conservatory breeds approximately 30 per cent of its own butterflies: 3,500 per month during

the summer and 1,500 to 2,000 monthly during the rest of the year. Between 12 and 15 butterfly species are raised in-house all year long. The number rises to more than 30 species during the summer, when there is more sunlight, which species such as the swallowtails need to complete their life cycle. Host plants, which are home to eggs and caterpillars, are also more plentiful, since some can be grown out of doors.

Inside the 650-square-metre (7,000-square-foot) greenhouses at the rear of the conservatory are the 40 breeding cages about the size of walk-in closets. A fine mesh screen covers each cage to keep caterpillars in — some are no bigger than a few grains of rice laid end to end — and other pests out.

For the most part, each species gets its own cage. Host plants such as the passion vine, popular with nearly every species, are placed on the racks inside of each cage, along with breeding pairs of butterflies. The number of pairs varies according to how many new specimens the conservatory needs to produce.

The butterflies lay their eggs on the leaves or sometimes the stalk of a host plant. When they hatch, the confined caterpillars — also known as larvae — begin feeding on the leaves of the host plants. Once they reach the pupae stage, they are collected and taken to the laboratory, where they are examined for disease and parasites and placed in

another set of cages or in the emergence window. When the pupae transform into butterflies, they are released into the conservatory.

It seems like a fairly simple but strict process, letting nature take its course while the conservatory provides a safe, clean, and comfortable habitat. Some species, however, are unable to reproduce in a contrived environment no matter how perfect the setting. It has been a hit-and-miss process with several species since the conservatory opened in 1996.

Butterflies whose host plants take a long time — in some cases two years — to grow back after being eaten by caterpillars are avoided. Breeding of the pretty, orange Julia butterfly was abandoned even though the conservatory was producing between 100 and 1,250 each week because it took too long for the host plant to re-grow its leaves. The entomology staff also take care to preserve genetic integrity by not letting too many generations of butterflies from the same mating pair continue breeding.

Another priority is making sure the caterpillars have enough food. New plants are added weekly to renew the food supply, while new host plants for some voracious eaters are replaced four times a week to provide enough nourishment. Some diets need a little enhancement. Puddles of salted water are added to the swallowtail breeding cages because this butterfly needs an

unusually large amount of salt to survive.

Since caterpillars are basically eating machines, munching and nibbling away at leaves until the plant is stripped bare, it's a certainty these little creatures produce a lot of frass, or caterpillar poop. Part of the strict breeding routine requires sweeping the floors each day to get rid of the frass. Black plastic tubing snakes through the greenhouse from cage to cage, providing water for each individual plant. By providing an automatic and continuous water supply, there is no need to spray the plants with hoses and run the risk of spreading the frass around.

Some species get special treatment. The Owl butterfly won't breed in the cages. Staff watch for Owls breeding in the conservatory and then move them back to the cages to lay the eggs.

A Cattleheart butterfly

Cattleheart butterflies can kill host plants, so the caterpillars are placed in plastic boxes filled with twigs. The Blue and White Longwing and the Tiger Longwing species were dropped from the breeding program because after going through the entire process, they would produce only five or six caterpillars. The Queen and Monarch butterflies are bred on a seasonal basis because their host plants grow best outdoors and are brought into the breeding cages as needed.

Inside the greenhouse, half of the structure is occupied by the production of passion vine for the breeding program. All of the longwings lay their eggs on this plant, which is also food for the larvae. The passion vine is grown continuously in 450 eight-litre (two-gallon) pots connected to metre-high (3-foot) trellises. Caterpillars strip the passion vine of its stems and dark purple-green leaves. It takes 12 weeks for the plant to re-grow its leaves.

Among the other plants kept in plentiful supply for the breeding program are the following:

- Ruellia melacosperma, which has purple flowers and long, narrow green leaves. It cannot be purchased commercially because it is considered a weed, but greenhouse staff started growing it from seed and later propogated it through cuttings.
- Citrus plants, such as miniature tangerine and lime, and calamondin orange trees and shrubs. About 50 of these plants are kept on hand. It takes three months for the leaves to grow back once decimated by caterpillars. The plants are kept in continuous production for three years, after which they die from exhaustion. New plants are imported from Florida. The plants are kept from growing fruit, which allows them to produce more leaves. (The calamondin is otherwise popular in making orange marmalade.)
- Prickly ash, a delicate-looking plant that is the favourite of the Giant Swallowtail. But as its branches and leaves are covered in prickly thorns, it is kept tucked away at the sides of the green-house to prevent injuries.
- Banana plant, crucial to the Owl breeding program. Since the Owl butterflies don't mate in the confines of the cages, a banana plant is kept in the conservatory. Any eggs laid on its leaves are transferred to other banana plants in the greenhouse cages.

CONSERVATORY RESEARCH

The conservatory's main goal is to showcase butterflies rather than make scientific advances. Nevertheless, some research is carried out. Entomologist Cheryl Tyndall, who is responsible for all the butterflies and the breeding program, is making headway in developing an artificial diet for caterpillars.

Working in a small, windowless room just off the conservatory laboratory, Tyndall has laid out dozens of tiny, translucent plastic cups on turquoise cafeteria trays. Lifting off the cover of each cup reveals tiny

Entomologist Cheryl Tyndall with soybean larva food medium

caterpillars climbing a mound of green paste that looks like dried-up modelling clay. This is their food.

The paste is pure protein made from a soybean base, with vitamins added to the mixture. To stimulate feeding, Tyndall has added ground-up pieces of leaves from the caterpillars' usual feeding plant. The smallest of the larvae, the newly hatched "neonates," are dropped gently into the cups to feed and grow on the artificial diet.

The Painted Lady, an orange, brown, and white butterfly familiar to southern Ontario, was the first to be raised successfully on the artificial diet. The results weren't surprising since the Painted Lady had already been raised on the diet elsewhere, but it gave Tyndall the experience needed to experiment with other species.

She moved on to the White Peacock, Buckeye, and Great Southern White to see if the caterpillars would begin feeding. The caterpillars ate the paste, but only five or six survived the initial test. After breeding the survivors, the larvae were put back immediately and exclusively on the artificial diet, the idea being that they would have inherited some type of genetic disposition towards the paste. Improvements have been gradual. Trial and error has shown that some larvae prefer tall plastic cups while others favour shorter and rounder containers. (There is no apparent explanation for these preferences.)

Staff have had no luck with the Atlas Moth, a massive 11-to 30-centimetre (4 3/4 to 12-inch-) wide species that is the only moth in the conservatory and available for only limited times of the year from butterfly farms in the Philippines. The moth requires lots of space and developed problems on the artificial diet.

However, Tyndall has become excited by advances in creating the right artificial diet for the spectacular Blue Morpho, one of the most popular butterflies anywhere because of its brilliant, shimmering blue colours. In the first experiments, three caterpillars reached the pupa stage and were pinned to corkboards to await the emergence of the butterfly. The silk thread produced by two pupae did not hold, and they fell to the floor and were damaged. A butterfly emerged from the third but was unable to open its wings.

The experiments to get just the right mixture of nutrients continue with the Blue Morpho. "We know we're on the right track," says Tyndall. "Now that we know it can be done, we will start collecting data and eventually we hope to publish the results."

Tyndall emphasizes that butterflies raised on the artificial diet or any others in the breeding program are never allowed outside of the conservatory. Because they have been bred and raised in a sterile environment, they are free of any predators and the threat of most diseases. They may not have the genetic qualities required to fight off disease in the outside world. If they were to breed

A Great Southern White

with other butterflies outside the conservatory, they might weaken the species' resistance to disease.

Tyndall believes the artificial diet program offers great advantages for the conservatory. It requires less space than breeding butterflies in the greenhouse cages and a smaller number of plants to provide part of the food supply. Any diseases can be confined to a single cup, reducing the threat of passing deadly illnesses on to caterpillars in other cups. It also saves the cost of electrical power and heating for the space the caterpillars would otherwise occupy in the greenhouse breeding cages.

"You can do a lot more with a lot less, but it takes a lot of effort to reach that point. It doesn't come easy," Tyndall says.

BUTTERFLY IMPORTS

Every Wednesday afternoon, a few sturdy boxes bearing the Niagara Falls Butterfly Conservatory address arrive by air freight at Pearson International Airport in Toronto from countries such as the Philippines and Costa Rica.

The shipments have become a familiar sight for Canada Customs and Agriculture Canada inspectors at the airport. Both must approve the shipments' entry to the country. A courier van awaiting the shipments is loaded with the boxes as soon as they are cleared by the inspectors and heads straight to the conservatory, a 150-kilometre (90-mile) trip that takes less than two hours.

The boxes, each about the size of a small suitcase, arrive at the conser-

vatory after the laboratory workday is done but while the building remains open to visitors. The shipment is carefully tucked away in a storage area behind the conservatory, where the boxes will safely remain all night, motionless but with the occasional rustling sound coming from inside.

Inside these boxes are the lifeblood of the conservatory:

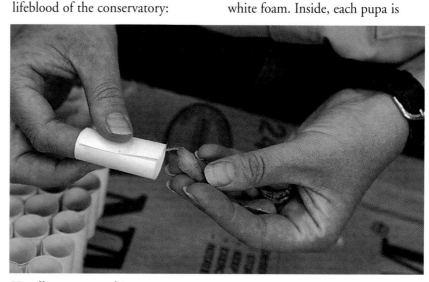

Handling a pupae shipment

hundreds of pupae from privately owned butterfly farms in the tropical regions of the world. Each box can hold as many as 1,000 pupae but normally contains between 500 and 600 of the sometimes already twitching specimens.

First thing Thursday morning, Cheryl Tyndall and the entomology staff open the boxes in the laboratory behind the emergence window and begin sorting through the dozens of different species.

About 70 per cent of the butterflies in the conservatory are imported. None are captured from the rainforest — all are raised on butterfly farms. The Costa Rican shipments arrive in ordinary brown cardboard boxes, the pupae individually wrapped. The Philippine supply comes more elaborately packaged. The cartons are made of stiff white foam. Inside, each pupa is

stuffed within a cardboard tube and cushioned with little puffs of cotton.

The pupae are first sorted by species. Each has its own distinctive markings, although most have a similar shape that has been described as resembling an almond or a human toe. The biggest pupa, at about 6 centimetres (2 1/4 inches) long, belongs to the Owl. Among the smallest is the green pupa of the Glasswing; the size of a fingertip, it produces a butterfly

A sorted and dated pupae shipment

with transparent wings.

Some pupae are as pretty as the butterflies themselves. The Rice Paper has a bright golden yellow pupa with black flecks. The pupa of the Broad Winged Mimic looks as if it were dipped in chrome and is attractive enough that some people have expressed a desire to wear them as earrings. The bright colours glitter in the lab but give the pupa a form of self-defence in the tropical rainforest by reflecting light and confusing predators about its location.

Other pupae can get quite active, twitching and shaking on the sorting table. The movement is contagious. When one starts moving, it sets off a chain reaction, and the rest of the pupae of the same species join in the dance.

"A lot of people think the pupa is an inactive resting stage, but there's a lot happening inside," Tyndall says.

Once the species are sorted, the serious job of inspecting each one for disease or parasite infestation

commences. Staff have learned from experience that the Common Mormon pupa is the most likely of any species to be infected by a parasitic wasp nearly microscopic in size. The normally green pupa becomes bloated and turns a salmon pink colour. The infected pupae are set aside to be destroyed by incineration, along with the cardboard and cotton packaging, which could also carry a tropical disease.

About 10 per cent of the pupae in any shipment are either infected, dead, damaged by rough handling, or in the stage of early butterfly emergence. Records are kept on the state of each pupa to track any developing

An interpreter and visitors at the emergence window

trends and to obtain reimbursement from the butterfly farms for dead or damaged pupae, which range in cost from $1.50 to $3 apiece.

There are several methods of tacking the pupae to the corkboards for display in the emergence window, where visitors can watch the butterfly come to life and shed the chrysalis. Some pupae arrive attached to a fragment of vegetation that can easily be pinned to the board. Other pupae spin a small piece of silk that can be secured to the board with a pin. Occasionally, visitors watching the work through the emergence window recoil when they see what looks like a staff member attacking a pupa with an electric glue gun. Some pupae have neither vegetation nor silk to work with, requiring the staff to glue a

piece of string on the pupa. A loop is made on the end of the string and pinned to the board without harming the pupa.

A Pharaoh Quail

INSECT CONTROL

There is a good reason for not using pesticides in the conservatory. Not only would the poison kill the unwanted bugs, but it would knock off the butterflies too. Butterflies are extremely sensitive to chemicals. One reason the conservatory is set back in a wooded area out of sight from the Niagara River Parkway is to keep automobile exhaust from drifting into the building and harming the butterflies.

Nevertheless, there is an ongoing war in the conservatory and greenhouses against all kinds of intruders. So far the horticultural staff have been winning with a battle strategy known as Integrated Pest Management. It means no chemicals are used to combat the invading insects. Instead, good bugs are set loose intentionally to conquer the bad bugs that have hitched a ride inside, usually on new plants.

Many of the plants were infested when they first arrived. By the time the conservatory opened in 1996, there were already three insect problems to be solved without resorting to pesticides. Discovered in the brand-new conservatory were spider mites, mealy bugs and scale, a round, flat, and transparent insect so small that it can't be seen until it spreads out across leaves and tree trunks, where it looks like a patch of fungus.

The problem with these three bugs was that they produced "honeydew," a sticky insect excrement that coats the leaves, causing mould to grow. The mould blocks sunlight, which causes the leaves to wither and die, leading to the death of the entire plant. In addition, the insects suck juices from the plant, contributing to its deterioration.

The spider mites were eliminated after staff released another form of mite, the Ambleysius Fallacis from British Columbia. Nobody knew if the mighty mite was doing its job until the spider mites disappeared. Since the attacking mites are too small to be seen, conservatory staff had to trust the shipment that arrived on a bean leaf. They simply set the leaf in the conservatory and waited for the nearly invisible mites to go to work.

About 200 small ladybugs, recognizable by their brown bodies and orange heads, are released inside the conservatory every week to battle the mealy bugs. The ladybug of choice, Cryptolaemus, is shipped from Europe.

Two types of friendly insects were brought in to take on the scale. Lindorus is a black ladybug the size of the tip of a ballpoint pen. The Lindorus lays eggs beneath the scale. The eggs, larvae, and adults all feed on the scale. The Metaphycus, a miniature wasp that is nearly invisible, also lays its eggs beneath the scale and begins munching away on the undesirable insect. The scale turns black and dies. Once their source of food is eliminated, the wasps also die off. The conservatory will likely never be without scale, so Lindorus and Metaphycus are regularly released inside.

A pair of local pests, the thrip and white fly, made their way into the greenhouses through the air vents and hitchhiked into the conservatory on plants. Without controls in place, each female thrip can reproduce 200 offspring every week. The tiny black bug goes through a crawling stage before becoming a flying insect. In both stages, the thrip kills leaves by sucking moisture from them. It also transmits the Tomato Spot Wilt virus — common in backyard gardens — and has infected several palm trees. The Orius, a pinhead-sized beetle with a hard shell and yellow diamond marking on its back, attacks the eggs and larvae of the thrip. However, the Orius beetles can't be used in the greenhouses because they would eat the caterpillars in the breeding cages. The thrip has left behind a legacy: the virus will remain permanently in the conservatory. The cost of merely testing for the virus is too expensive at $60 to $90 per plant.

The local white fly infested the Porter Weed, the most common plant grown in the greenhouse. White flies often find their way into people's homes aboard poinsettia plants during the Christmas season. The Encarsia, a tiny wasp about the size of a pen dot, lays its eggs inside the scale created by the white fly, turning it black and killing it.

Since none of the plants inside the conservatory are considered appropriate hosts for butterfly eggs, no one anticipated caterpillars as a problem. But the Owl species unexpectedly laid eggs that hatched into leaf-crunching caterpillars. Sometimes the eggs are just blasted by the power washer used to clean the conservatory. Occasionally they can be picked by hand from an overhanging leaf, then bagged, frozen, and sent for incineration. But most of the work is done by Podisius, the biggest bug, (slightly larger than a local ladybug) let loose in the conservatory. About 100 Podisius bugs are let loose each week. They pierce the skin of the caterpillar and devour the insides. Extra care must be taken to keep the Podisius from getting out of the conservatory and into the breeding cages in the greenhouses.

Ants and cockroaches are additional problems. Horticulturist Judy Colley whipped up a mixture of molasses and bran that solved the ant problem but couldn't keep up with the rapidly growing population of Australian cockroaches. Trying to control the cockroach, which existed before the dinosaur and is able to survive conditions fatal to many forms of life, is difficult. More than 140 lengths of plastic pipe have been hidden throughout the conservatory, each containing a piece of commercial cockroach killer. When the first piece of pipe containing a three-month supply was set out, the gel bait was gone within a week. But there was a noticeable drop in the number of cockroaches.

Finally, the small birds that dart between the bushes manage to help out with insect disposal. The Pharaoh quails eat the dead butterflies that are out of reach of the clean-up crews.

The Building

above
The conservatory exterior

right
Visitors enjoying an exhibit in the lobby

Glass, glass, and more glass. That's what a butterfly house is made of. And presumably, that would be the first thought of any architect interested in designing a conservatory.

Instead, the Niagara Parks Butterfly Conservatory grew from an old pile of stone. Architect Barry Sampson recalls tramping through the long grass of an overgrown nursery behind the Niagara Parks Commission botanical gardens on his way to the proposed site of the conservatory.

There he discovered a simple stone wall built from stacked slabs of limestone without the use of mortar or cement. Students at the commission's neighbouring Niagara Parks School of Horticulture had unearthed the stones as they worked in the gardens. They had assembled the wall over several decades, inspired by the traditional layered stone fences fronting the grand homes along the Niagara River between the historic villages of Queenston and Niagara-on-the-Lake.

"We were quite interested in that wall because it was made from the actual stone of the Niagara

Escarpment. In the botanical gardens this was the only location where it occurred. That made us think much of the building should be made from stone, and it should have some of the qualities you find in Niagara," says Sampson, a partner in the Toronto architectural firm Baird/Sampson/Neuert, which was selected by the parks commission to design the 1,022 square-metre (11,000 square-foot) conservatory.

Glass could wait. The architects now had their vision. The biggest conservatory in North America would not only house butterflies but serve as a tribute to the natural history of the region, including its waterfall.

Barry Sampson and George Baird were co-directors of the project. Partner Jon Neuert became project architect soon after. All three would contribute ideas that helped create the startling shape that evolved during the design process.

CREATING THE COCOON

The final drawings for the conservatory revealed it would be built in the form of a chrysalis, the cocoon stage in the life of a butterfly. The evolving design had resulted in a structure that was both efficiently functional and pleasing to the eye, much like a butterfly itself.

And then there came a snag. Fifty tonnes of roughly cut limestone were needed to build the front wall and entrance to the conservatory. Although the area is largely

composed of limestone, none was available locally. The Niagara Escarpment is a narrow ribbon of limestone that starts in nearby Queenston and winds its way northwest to the Bruce Peninsula, which separates Lake Huron from Georgian Bay. The escarpment is a unique landform given special ecological status by the United Nations. Much of it, especially in the urbanized parts of the Niagara Peninsula, is protected from development. Rock quarries in the Niagara region no longer exist.

The search expanded to the north until the right kind of limestone was found in a quarry near the small town of Wiarton at the bottom of the Bruce Peninsula. In addition to the front of the conservatory, the

limestone was used to build the wall around the facility's outdoor garden — a space filled with flowers, bushes, and shrubs that attract native butterflies.

The sloped glass walls and roof of the conservatory rise from behind the front wall to create what *Canadian Architect* magazine described as "two essentially nineteenth century architectural types: the picturesque pavilion (or ruin) in the garden evoked by a series of rustic stone walls, and the Victorian glass house."

Although the conservatory is one of the finest structures in Niagara Falls, it is hidden behind a stand of trees within the botanical gardens. That was no accident.

"From the beginning, the idea was that the conservatory would be

a part of the entire botanical garden experience. It was not going to be showcased as a roadside attraction. The idea was to enhance the garden," Sampson says.

Before the conservatory was built, the botanical gardens attracted about 500,000 people each year. Parks Commission officials believed

would become the main attraction, with the botanical gardens playing a secondary role. More than 600,000 people have visited the conservatory each year since it opened, and the number keeps climbing. The gardens are now a place to take a stroll while waiting for the designated time stamped on an

hands-on displays featuring butterfly facts and a sampling of trivia.

A pair of small theatres show a video of the conservatory. This provides another form of crowd control, staggering the entrance of visitors to the butterfly house and preventing gridlock along the paths. Despite the huge number of visitors, the conservatory rarely feels crowded. That, too, was part of the design.

After taking on the project, Sampson and Baird travelled to several butterfly conservatories in the United States and found some common problems. The buildings were tall, to give the butterflies enough space to fly, but visitors on the flat ground-level floors had a difficult time viewing the soaring butterflies high overhead.

The interior winding path

the conservatory would add to the experience of walking through the pleasant gardens, themselves a welcome reprieve from the crowds thronging to the edge of the Horseshoe Falls and the carnival-like atmosphere of Clifton Hill.

TAKING THE TOUR
The Parks Commission did not anticipate that the conservatory

admission ticket to the conservatory.

Once inside the front door, visitors encounter the first change made to the original building, carried out within a year of its opening. A multi-purpose auditorium wasn't getting as much use as expected, while the lobby had quickly become overcrowded. The auditorium was removed and an entertaining information centre installed, with several

The answer was to create a three-dimensional experience, where winding paths lead from a "valley floor" near the entrance to the top of the conservatory and the edge of a 6-metre-high (20-foot) waterfall. The hilly interior of the conservatory was constructed from 800 tonnes of granite extracted near the French River, the route of the original fur traders, about 500 kilometres (300 miles) to the north.

"You rise to the metaphorical crest of a hill that gives you a view of the entire landscape. You walk up from a flat level and it is an unfolding experience," Neuert says.

The building sits on a north-south line to take best advantage of the

Visitors at the conservatory waterfall

sunshine. It is low and wide at one end and narrow and tall at the other. The layout of the walkways through the lush tropical foliage creates the impression that the conservatory is bigger than it really is.

"It is an effective planning tool for orchestrating large numbers of people through it. The different paths contained by the rock means no one is ever at eye-level with anyone else in other parts of the conservatory," Neuert explains.

THE INNER WORKINGS

Glass houses provide a challenge for the technical components of a building, such as electrical wiring,

plumbing, and heating and cooling systems. There are no walls to hide them behind. The only obvious mechanical devices in the conservatory are the small chrome nozzles sticking up through the garden beds, which deliver a fine mist from a high-pressure watering system that keeps the humidity at a constant 75 per cent. The conservatory is kept at 27°C (80°F) during the day and a few degrees cooler at night, when the butterflies are less active. High-intensity lights augment natural sunshine, especially in winter, when northern daylight hours are considerably shorter than in the tropics.

Heating and cooling pipes and

vents have been skilfully hidden inside the rock — with visitors feeling an occasional gust of air from a vent camouflaged by the foliage. The ventilation system is powerful, with the ability to change 8,500 cubic metres (300,000 cubic feet) of air within a minute. In summer, rows of vents in the walls and ceiling can be opened when the conservatory heats up under the sun, allowing hot air to escape through the top while drawing cooler air in at the bottom and reducing dependency on air conditioning.

During the winter, when the temperature outdoors can plunge well below freezing, condensation on the windows is a potential problem. Any water forming on the window slides down into a drip container, preventing spontaneous outbreaks of indoor rainfall.

The white netting that lines the conservatory helps control the flow of air, so the butterflies are not caught up in turbulence. It prevents the butterflies from sticking to the wet windows in winter. It is also part of a double barrier — the other part is the glass — required by federal laws to prevent any tropical species from escaping the facility.

Every mechanical function within the conservatory is controlled by computer including opening the vents, activating the heating and cooling systems to control temperature, determining when the misting nozzles will begin spraying, and activating the lights when darkness sets in. The computer is programmed to guarantee an optimal environment for the survival of the butterflies. It also acts as an electrical watchdog. Should the power fail in the building, especially overnight when no one is around, the computer will automatically start a diesel-powered generator to keep everything running.

The computer turns on the lights when darkness sets in. If the butterflies do not get enough light, they will enter a dormant stage called diapause, a form of hibernation, and remain inactive for months. The

double-glazed glass windows, with argon gas trapped between the layers as an insulator, are not tinted, allowing for a maximum amount of light penetration. The architects discovered that some conservatories in warmer climates had tinted the glass to deflect heat, but the reduced amount of sunlight made for sluggish butterflies.

BRANCHING OUT

Parts of the conservatory are purely efficient — such as the lamination on the glass that causes a broken window to crumble like automobile glass, instead of shattering into dangerous shards. Others are more cleverly functional.

Holy Wood Lignum Vitae

The interior steel structure was designed to resemble the branches of a tree reaching out to support the building. The catwalk running down the centre beneath the glass ceiling allows access for maintenance work and provides support to the steel columns, preventing the building from collapsing under its own weight.

The steel supports are both galvanized and painted white to resist corrosion. The constant high level of humidity presents a greater threat of rust indoors than the environment outside. The design won the Ontario Steel Design Award from the Canadian Institute of Steel Construction Association, beating out the 93,000-square-metre (1-million-square-foot) National Trade Centre at Toronto's Exhibition Place.

Indeed, practically everything about the conservatory has turned out precisely as the architects envisioned. Except for one thing. Few visitors see the building as representing a chrysalis. Most tell the conservatory staff that the building looks like a boat, an impression that evokes the image of a Noah's Ark for butterflies, voyaging amid environmental degradation around the world.

Occasionally a visitor pictures the conservatory as a barn. The architects can live with that interpretation. "We don't see that as a negative because that is another form of agrarian use," Neuert says.

The Plant Species

Butterflies cannot survive without plants. They live in them and feed on them. Plants also provide a spot for the butterfly to lay its eggs.

There are more than 90 different plant species within the conservatory, about one-third more trees, bushes, and flowers than there are species of butterflies.

Here are 12 plants that horticulturist Judy Colley believes are essential to the butterfly conservatory.

Scarlet Bush
Hamelia patens

Nectar comes gushing from these flowers when they are squeezed. The conservatory has about 15 of these plants with little orange flowers that resemble tiny tubes of lipstick cascading from the bush. Numerous butterflies can feed on the flowers at the same time. The plant continues to flower all year long providing the butterflies with a never-ending supply of food.

Porter Weed
Stachytarpheta frantsii

There are hundreds of nectar-rich Porter Weed plants throughout the conservatory. It is the most common and plentiful food source for butterflies. Known around the conservatory simply as "stachy," it puts out new flowers every few days during the summer. In winter, the plants are replaced every few weeks from a reserve supply grown in the conservatory's greenhouse to ensure a constant supply of nectar. Porter Weed is a small, green bush with hairy, sap-covered leaves and blue flowers that look like candlesticks sitting on top of a long stalk.

Australian Tree Fern
Cyathea cooperi

Visitors pass this huge tree as soon as they walk through the entrance to the conservatory. A special permit from the Canadian government was required before this tree could be obtained because it is on the endangered list of plants protected by the Convention on International Trade in Endangered Species. The woody centre of the trunk is just 5 centimetres (2 inches) in diameter, but it is wrapped in thick roots that grow up the side of the tree. (Staff water the trunk, not the ground.) Overnight, many of the butterflies roost in the tree, hanging upside down from its fronds. It is especially popular with the Owl butterfly.

Sago Palm
Cycas revolta

The two Sago Palms in the conservatory were already between 80 and 100 years old when they arrived in 1996. Standing from 3 to 5 metres (10 to 16 feet) tall, this slow-growing tree originated millions of years before flowering plants. It is capable of storing water within its trunk for more than a year to withstand drought, and it is considered dioecious, meaning the palm can be either male or female. Butterflies roost at night beneath the fronds.

Holy Wood Lignum Vitae

Guaiacum sanctum

The wood from this tree is so dense that it will sink if submerged in salt water. It was once prized for the manufacture of expensive croquet mallets and balls and also used centuries ago for pegs to hold together planks in sailing ships. This tree grows wider than it does tall. Even though the two Holy Woods are the smallest trees in the conservatory, they are the most expensive, costing about $1,500 apiece. It is a colourful tree, with orange pods covering red seeds and brilliant blue flowers with yellow stamens that resemble African violets. The flowers provide nectar for the butterflies.

Garland Flower

Hedychium coronarium

In Hawaii, the wonderfully fragrant flowers of this plant are used to make the traditional leis that are draped around the necks of visitors. The colour of the flower varies from a creamy white to various shades of red. It is sometimes called "the poor man's orchid." It has been planted near the conservatory waterfall because it thrives in bogs and swamps. It can grow to be about 2.5 metres (8 feet) tall. The flower is shaped like a cup at the bottom and collects nectar, which the butterflies drink. After the plant flowers, it must be cut back like a corn stalk before it will blossom again.

Orange Jessamine

Murraya paniculata

When this shrub is in bloom near the top of the conservatory, it is so fragrant it can be smelled all the way to the rear door. Also known as Satin Wood, the shrub is more than 2 metres (6 1/2 feet) around, with silvery bark and glossy, forest green leaves. Butterflies feed on the red berries and the nectar of the clusters of white, trumpet-shaped flowers.

Common Screw Pine
Pandanus utilis

This large tree is located across from the emergence window, where visitors gather to watch butterflies coming out of the pupae. The long, woody tendrils that shoot out from the trunk and set in the ground are actually roots used as anchors to keep the tree from tipping over. The cannon-ball-sized fruit produced by the tree resembles a large, round pineapple but is not edible. Anyone getting down on the ground and looking straight up into the tree will notice that the branches and leaves create a spiral pattern all the way to the top. However, the leaves are extremely sharp and can easily cut anyone who sticks a hand into the tree. Butterflies can hide themselves from predators (although none exist in the conservatory) on the tree, and the Owl species camouflages itself against the trunk.

Weeping Bottlebrush
Callistemon viminalis

These five trees stand about 9 metres (30 feet) tall. Angled across from one another, they form a canopy above the conservatory entrance. The tiny leaves are green on one side and silver on the other. Dead branches are left on the trees because longwing butterflies use them as a roosting spot. Rice Paper butterflies feed on the small red flowers that look like brushes for scrubbing bottles.

Richmond Red Wild Plantain
Heliconia caribea
and
Hanging Lobster Claw
Heliconia rostrata

These two flowering plants are similar in every way but one. The Wild Plantain produces a rowboat-shaped red basket weighing up to 7 kilograms (15 pounds) that holds flowers in an upright position. The spiky yellow flowers produce nectar, and butterflies feed by sitting on the edge of the "boat." It is one of the tallest plants in the conservatory, stretching up more than 12 metres (39 feet). The Hanging Lobster Claw reaches the same height, but its baskets of flowers hang upside down.

Burmese Fishtail Palm
Caryota mitis

The trunk of this palm appears to be covered in a fishnet stocking because of the woven strands of bark that cover the tree. The leaves themselves have a triangular shape and look like schools of fish. The yellow flower it produces cascades down like a horse's tail. Butterflies feed on the pollen. The flower can produce up to 1,250 millilitres (5 cups) of pollen every day. The easiest way to find this tree in the conservatory is to look for a staff member sweeping up pollen from the floor with a broom. Brown seeds as big as nickles hang from the ends of the "horse tails." like ornaments on a Christmas tree.

Poinciana
Caesalpina granadilla

Butterflies rest on the trunk and in the branches of this most unusual tree. At the best of times, the Poinciana looks in poor health, especially in the spring when it drops all of its leaves. (Most people in Canada and the United States are familiar with hardwood trees losing leaves in the fall.) Although it looks dead, it isn't. The trunk has a mottled appearance because the tree exfoliates (or sheds) patches of its bark, giving it varying shades of green. At night the leaves look wilted, as if they are ready to die. In fact, they merely curl up in the evening to retain warmth and moisture.

The Butterfly Garden

Landscape architect Janet Rosenberg took one look at the plans for the butterfly conservatory and made a single demand: push the building back 8 metres (25 feet) to make room for a butterfly garden. Fortunately, conservatory construction had not yet started and she got her way.

Rosenberg designed the butterfly garden surrounding the entrance to the conservatory. The goal was to attract as many of the 150 butterfly species native to Ontario as possible.

The plan seems to be working. During the first summer, when the garden was still being developed, an informal log of sightings kept by the conservatory's observatory staff revealed that 10 species of butterflies stopped to take in some nectar. The following summer, 25 species were spotted, and the number of total butterflies was on the rise.

In addition to the large number of Monarchs, Cabbage White, and Common Sulphurs, the garden has attracted plenty of other standouts, among them the Red Admiral, Mourning Cloak, Comma (shaped just like its name), Canadian Tiger Swallowtail, and the Black Swallowtail.

A low, limestone slab wall encloses more than 120 flowering

The Butterfly Garden

plants, shrubs, and small trees, selected for their ability to attract butterflies. The stone wall provides shelter on windy days and a ledge where the butterflies can warm themselves and replenish their energy so they can continue flying. The garden is at the east end of the conservatory, where it can obtain the most light early in the day.

Most of the flowering plants are perennials; they blossom year after year. The plants most popular with the butterflies are the varieties of the aptly named Butterfly Bush, with its pink or dark purple, long, trumpet-

A Cabbage White

A flowering Butterfly Bush

like flowers, says horticulturist Jennifer Voogt. Other butterfly magnets include the Purple Coneflower and both pink and white phlox.

The garden reaches its peak colours in June, but plants were selected to allow the garden to remain in flower from spring through fall. The fragrant white flower of the Hydrangea shrub and the Tree Lilacs appear in spring, Bugbane flowers through July and August, and the New England Aster with its purple flowers with yellow centres in late September.

Voogt, a graduate of the adjacent Niagara Parks School of Horticulture, oversees the care of the garden. She has at least one big advantage over other local gardeners. The hard clay soil typical of the Niagara Peninsula was excavated and replaced with high-grade topsoil to ensure a lush garden.

TRY THIS AT HOME

Creating a backyard butterfly garden is fairly easy for amateur gardeners. And there's no need to replace the soil.

"It's not difficult at all," Rosenberg advises. "As long as you have some basic gardening skills and can tell the difference between short and tall plants that attract butterflies, it is actually pretty easy."

What exactly, then, is a butterfly garden? It is a section of your yard that receives plenty of sun, is sheltered from the wind (which can be accomplished with some tall plants) and filled with the type of nectar-producing flowers that will attract butterflies. There will be caterpillars if the plants selected are suitable for the larvae to feed upon.

Although attractive, it will not be a traditional garden. It will not contain roses, irises, or tulips, which are popular in most gardens but of no interest to butterflies. It will have to be kept free of pesticides because chemicals are fatal to butterflies. In fact, it is helpful to stop using pesticides even in areas that are near the garden.

Butterfly-garden experts insist the first step is not turning the soil and getting ready for planting. You should start by spending some time — the experts suggest a few hours during the middle of the day (when butterflies are most active) for a period of several sunny days — observing the types of butterflies in your neighbourhood. This will help you decide which flowers to plant.

Next you should select your site. It should get five or six hours of sunshine daily and be out of the way of heavy-traffic areas such as where children play.

The next step is to select your plants. If you choose only nectar-producing flowers, you can expect butterflies to stop by for a snack. Adding larval food plants will give the butterflies a reason to stay around, reproduce, and lay eggs. Consideration must also be given to geography. A butterfly garden in Ontario or the United States around the Great Lakes will be different than a similar garden in Florida because of the change in seasons. Any reputable butterfly gardening book will contain a list of plants suitable for the varying geographic regions of North America.

GETTING THE RIGHT PLANTS

Some fundamentals are appropriate to all regions. Shorter plants should be arranged in the front of the garden, and the taller varieties in the rear. Plants that bloom in the same colour should be planted in clusters. Larval food plants should not be front and centre. Try to select plants that will bloom at different times throughout the spring, summer, and fall to provide colour during the entire growing season.

In Ontario, suitable plants include clover or periwinkle for ground cover, annuals such as marigolds, petunias, and zinnias, and perennials such as coneflowers, daisies, and phlox. If you have the room, shrubs such as azalea, Butterfly Bush, and lilac also work well. Cherry, pear, and plum trees are other welcome additions.

Although considered a noxious weed, milkweed makes an ideal plant because it is a host for numerous butterflies, including the Monarch. Incorporating milkweed is easier said than done. The milkweed plant is practically impossible to transplant because of its long taproot.

Some accessories around the garden will also help attract butterflies and encourage them to take up residence. Low-lying spots can be kept wet or turned into puddles to create a source of drinking water. Fieldstones give butterflies a place to bask in the sun. Pieces of fruit left on feeding dishes are another incentive.

Don't set your expectations too high. Like the conservatory, in Ontario you can expect to see Monarchs, Cabbage Whites, and Common Sulphurs. But even the

Joe Pye Weed

best gardens do not attract hordes of butterflies.

So why bother? Conservation is one good reason. The wood lots, open fields, and meadows favoured by butterflies have mostly been destroyed in Canada, the United States, and Europe. Planting this type of garden is one small way of trying to recreate the butterfly's natural habitat.

Janet Rosenberg and Associates of Toronto have developed a plan for a butterfly garden which you can try in your own backyard. It is reproduced on the following two pages of this book. The garden, which can be adapted to your own needs, is based on a typical rectangular urban lot and includes trees, shrubs, and perennials that are suitable for sunny, southern Canadian locations.

There are also a large number of books on butterfly gardening available at libraries and bookstores. Some that would help you get started include *Butterfly Gardening: Creating a Butterfly Haven in Your Garden*, by Thomas C. Emmel (1997); *The Butterfly Garden: Turning Your Garden, Window Boxes or Backyard into a Beautiful Home for Butterflies*, by Mathew Tekulsky (1985); *Grow a Butterfly Garden*, by Wendy P. Springer (1990); *Creating a Butterfly Garden*, by Marcus H. Schneck (1994); and *The National Wildlife Federation Guide to Gardening for Wildlife*, by Craig Tufts and Peter H. Loewer (1995).

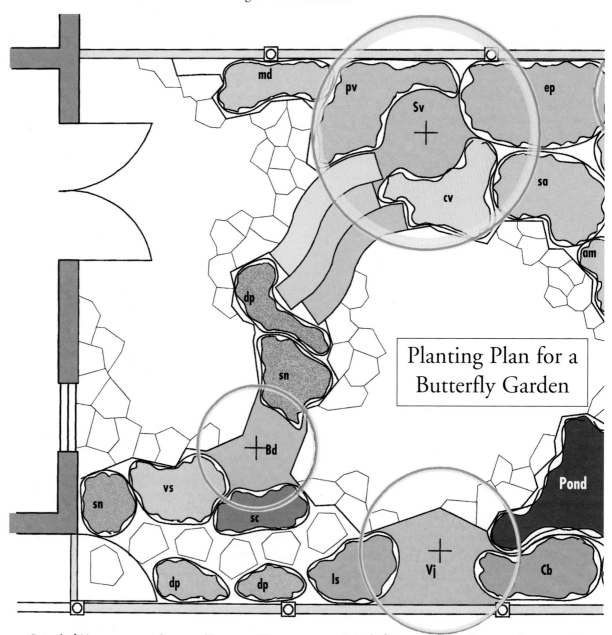

Planting Plan for a Butterfly Garden

		Botanical Name	Common Name	Zone
Trees:	Cc	Carpinus caroliniana	Blue Beech	3-9
	Ap	Aesculus parviflora	Bottlebrush Buckeye	4-8
	Bd	Buddleia davidii 'cv.'	Butterfly-bush	5-9
	Cb	Caryopteris x c landonensis 'cv.'	Blue-mist Shrub	6-9
Shrubs:	Co	Cephalanthus occidentalis	Buttonbush	5-10
	Ca	Clethra alnifolia 'Paniculata'	Summersweet Clethra	3-9
	Lb	Lindera benzoin	Spicebush	4-9
	Sv	Syringa vulgaris 'cv.'	Common Lilac	3-8
	Vj	Viburnum x juddii	Judd Viburnum	4-8

	Botanical Name	Common Name	Zone
ay	Achillea millefolium 'cv.'	Common Yarrow	2-9
af	Agastache foeniculum 'cv.'	Anise-Hyssop	2-9
am	Anaphalis margaritacea	Pearly Everlasting	2-9
al	Artemesia ludoviciana 'Silver King'	Silver Sage	4-9
at	Asclepias tuberosa	Butterfly Weed	4-9
as	Aster sp.	Aster	3-9
ac	Astilbe chinensis 'cv.'	Chinese Astilbe	3-9
cp	Campanula persicifolia	Peach-leaved Bellflower	2-9
co	Chelone obliqua	Turtlehead	3-9

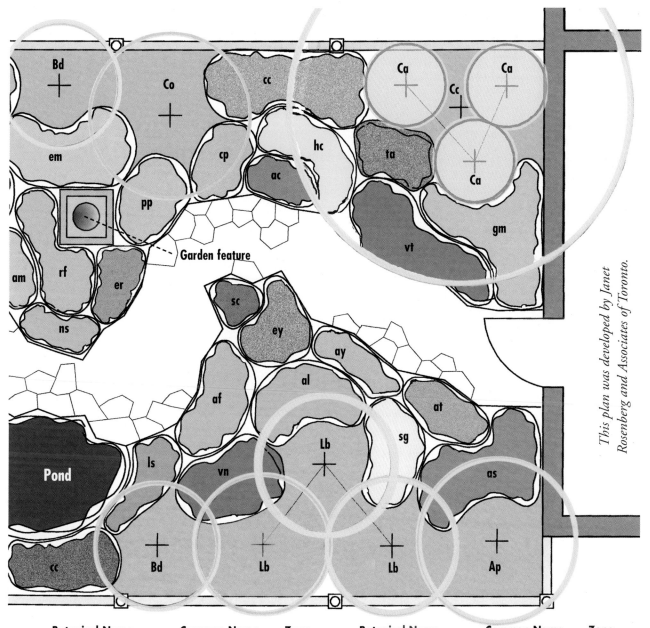

Garden feature

Pond

This plan was developed by Janet Rosenberg and Associates of Toronto.

	Botanical Name	Common Name	Zone		Botanical Name	Common Name	Zone
cv	Coreopsis verticillata 'cv.'	Thread-leaved Coreopsis	3-9	ns	Nepeta sibirica 'cv.'	Siberian Catmint	3-9
cc	Crambe cordifolia	Sea Kale	5-9	pp	Phlox paniculata 'cv.'	Garden Phlox	3-9
dp	Dianthus plumarius 'cv.'	Cottage Pinks	3-9	pv	Physostegia virginiana 'cv.'	Obedient Plant	2-9
ep	chinacea purpurea	Purple Coneflower	3-9	rf	Rudbeckia fulgida 'Goldstrum'	Cone-flower	3-9
er	Echinops ritro	Globe Thistle	2-9	sn	Salvia nemerosa 'cv.'	Perennial Salvia	3-9
ey	Eryngium yuccifolium	Rattlesnake Master	4-9	sc	Scabiosa columbaria 'cv.'	Pincushion Flower	3-9
em	Eupatorium maculatum 'Atropurpureum'	Joe-Pye Weed	4-9	sa	Sedum 'Autumn Joy'	Autumn Joy Sedum	2-9
gm	Geranium maculatum	Spotted Cranesbill	4-9	sg	Solidago 'cv.'	Golden-Rod	2-9
hc	Hemerocallis 'cv.'	Daylily	2-9	ta	Thalictrum aquilegifolium	Columbine Meadow-rue	3-9
ls	Liatris spicata 'cv.'	Blazing Star	2-9	vn	Vernonia novebaracensis	Ironweed	4-9
md	Monarda didyma 'cv.'	Bee-Balm	3-9	vs	Veronica spicata 'cv.'	Spike Speedwell	2-9
				vl	Viola labradorica	Purple Labrador Violet	4-9

Perennials:

The Environmental Threat

top
*A Banded Orange butterfly:
the natural habitat for many
species is fast disappearing*

right
*The Monarch butterfly is
endangered in all ten
provinces*

Our planet has lost 38 butterfly species to extinction, and another 159 are on the endangered list produced by The World Conservation Union.

But that tells only a portion of the story. The conservation union's list, although prepared through rigorous scientific study and evaluation, is far from complete. According to endangered lists created within individual countries, there are many more species whose numbers are tumbling to dangerously low levels and who could possibly become extinct unless measures are taken to preserve their existence.

While butterflies have many natural enemies, only humans are capable of the kind of widespread destruction that could eliminate an entire species.

In the United States, 19 of the 575 types of indigenous butterflies are considered endangered, according to the federal Fish and Wildlife Department. The conservation union lists just 5 in the United States but notes another 35 are extinct. The Canadian Wildlife Service of Environment Canada has placed 5 of the 275 species in this country on the endangered list. The conservation union so far has listed only one.

Those endangered in Canada include the Frosted Elfin and Karner Blue in Ontario, the Island Marble in British Columbia, the Maritime Ringlet in Quebec and New Brunswick, and the Monarch in all 10 provinces.

You won't find a Karner Blue at the Niagara conservatory. You likely won't find one anywhere in Ontario, where it is considered "extirpated," meaning it has not been seen for years and is most likely extinct.

What happened to the Karner Blue is typical of the threat faced by thousands of butterflies around the world. The Karner Blue lost its home: humans took it away. The Karner Blue relied on a tall, thin, purple flower — the Wild Lupine — to survive. Twice a year, the butterfly laid eggs on the leaves of the plant, and the caterpillars fed on the leaves. The butterfly never travelled more than a few hundred metres in a day and lived its short 10-day life within a small area around the food source.

The Wild Lupine grows in dry, usually sandy soil in open wooded areas. Precious little exists today, although some community groups plant the flower, hoping to restore the Karner Blue species. Across southern Ontario and the northern United States, practically all of the Karner Blue habitat has been ploughed under for farms, paved over to build roads, or covered by houses, factories, office towers, and shopping malls.

In the United States, about the only place you'll find this tiny blue butterfly — roughly the size of a quarter — is in The Pine Bush, a small woods constantly under the threat of housing development in Albany, New York. Local environmental activists are regularly in court to preserve the wood lot.

The developed countries of the world have a disgraceful record when it comes to protecting butterfly species. The Monarch is probably the most striking example.

The Monarch makes its home in Canada, the United States, and Mexico. It is the official symbol of the Commission for Environmental Cooperation, the ecological watchdog agency set up among the three countries under the North American Free Trade Agreement.

The Monarch is prized by residents of all three countries, who rejoice in glimpsing one of the familiar orange-and-black specimens or large clusters migrating each fall from Canada and the United States to Mexico and returning each spring.

With as many as 100 million Monarchs travelling the migratory

route, it is hard to believe that the Monarch could be considered a potentially endangered species. But it is. In Canada and the United States, development has wiped out much of the natural habitat for this species. The Monarch requires the milkweed plant, on which the caterpillars feed, to survive. But the amount of milkweed is dwindling as cities expand. Ground-level ozone, the major component in smog, kills milkweed. Even when thriving, milkweed is purposely destroyed because it is considered a noxious weed. In rural areas where crops are sprayed, it can absorb pesticides that are fatal to butterflies.

And there is a newer threat in the form of genetically altered food, the controversial technique of changing the characteristics of one plant by the addition of genes from another.

One "success" story in this field has been the addition of a gene known as BT to corn. BT is an organic pesticide with the ability to kill caterpillars and other larvae that invade a cornfield. This reduces the need for farmers to spray chemical pesticides. However, milkweed flourishes near cornfields. Research at Cornell University in Corning, New York has shown that the pollen from corn altered with the BT substance is fatal to the Monarch caterpillar. Although field tests have not been conducted, leading some industry officials to say there is no proof of a threat, corn pollen can easily spread on the wind to nearby milkweed plants.

In Mexico, the Monarch spends the winter at no more than 14 resting spots in the forests of the Transvolcanic Mountains region. Millions of butterflies roost in each of the small locations, making them especially vulnerable to destruction. In 1992 and 1995 unusually cold winters that included snowfalls killed as many as 5 million butterflies in each of the two years. The forests are also threatened with destruction. Only five sites are protected from logging. The oyamel tree, where the Monarchs roost, is harvested for lumber. Other areas are cleared for agriculture and cattle grazing.

For butterflies in general, the greatest threat lies in the tropical regions of the world. The vast majority of butterfly species — numbering in the thousands — live in tropical rainforests that are being destroyed at an astounding rate.

In the Philippines, where butterfly farms export many species to the conservatory, 1,800 hectares (4,500 acres) of forest are lost every day. The country's valued hardwood forests have been reduced to a remaining 700,000 hectares (1.7 million acres) from 16 million hectares (39.5 million acres). The butterfly habitat there is dwindling fast.

Butterflies need the tropical rainforest to survive. Over the past 20 years, 300 million hectares (740 million acres) — six times the size of France — of tropical forest has vanished to make way for agricultural use.

In all, 5 million hectares (12 million acres) of forest are logged each year throughout the world's tropical regions. Every tree that is cut down causes the loss of much more butterfly habitat. The rainforest is so dense that only about 10 per cent of the trees are actually harvested. But their removal pokes holes in the canopy created by the towering trees, which protects all the vegetation closer to the ground. As a result, between 30 and 60 per cent of the non-commercial trees subsequently die.

Much more rainforest is destroyed to accommodate cattle grazing in order to meet the immense demand for beef — mostly hamburgers — in the fast food society of the developed countries. It takes 6.25 square metres (67 square feet) of cleared rainforest to make a single quarter-pound hamburger, based on the amount of weight gained by a single head of cattle over eight years of grazing in the tropics before it is sent for slaughter.

Although it might seem insignificant, the third biggest demand on wood in tropical regions is for cooking fuel. Nearly 2 billion people in developing countries collect wood to prepare meals. Each individual uses an average of nearly 0.5 cubic metres (17 1/2 cubic feet) each year, an amount equal to all the paper products used annually by an individual in the developed world.

Global warming is the next big challenge for butterflies. An international study has found that numerous butterfly species in Europe have moved north, possibly as a result of the increasing temperature of the planet caused by a build-up of greenhouse gas emissions in the atmosphere. Butterflies are extremely sensitive to changes in the climate.

The study, which involved butterfly experts from across Europe and the United States, found 22 of the 35 species studied had either died out or moved between 30 and 240 kilometres (19 and 150 miles) beyond their previous northern ranges. For instance, the Sooty Copper butterfly (Heodes tityrus) disappeared from Spain and was discovered in Estonia.

At the University of California, researchers found recently that the Edith's Checkerspot butterfly population in Mexico is dwindling, as the average annual temperature is creeping upward. Larger numbers of the same butterfly were found along the Pacific coast in the northwestern United States and in western Canada.

The World Conservation Union issued this warning in a special report marking the end of the twentieth century: "The world's species (including butterflies) face an unprecedented crisis. The rate at which they are being lost is alarming even when compared with the extinction episode 70 million years ago when the dinosaurs disappeared…. The rate of extinction also appears to be increasing. Species are threatened in every habitat and on every continent, though the severity of threat varies from place to place."

"There are many causes of the current extinction crisis," the report concludes, "but all of them stem from the unsustainable management of the planet by humans."